Love Moves Us Forward

reflections on
kindness, connection, and peace

Patty Boo-Pryor

This work includes various translations of
Saint Francis de Sales' writings that have been
adapted and paraphrased into modern English.

ISBN: 978-1-7364388-0-0
First Edition: February 2021
Heart House Press LLC

Love is [the heart's] action. . . .
Love makes it move forward. . . .
Love is its flight. . . .
To put it clearly and precisely,
love is simply the movement, outpouring, and progress
of the heart towards the good.
Treatise on the Love of God
by Saint Francis de Sales

dedication

This book is dedicated to the Visitation Sisters
who taught, inspired, and shaped
four generations of women in my family.

CONTENTS

introduction

Love Moves Us Forward is based on the writings of Saint Francis de Sales (1567 – 1622). Saint Francis de Sales was co-founder of the Visitation Order (with Saint Jane de Chantal), Bishop of Geneva, a writer, a spiritual director, and a friend to many. Throughout his works, he emphasized that spirituality begins in the heart and is expressed through one's words and actions. In his numerous letters of spiritual direction, he offered advice on growing closer to God and serving others wherever one may find oneself, suggesting that one's spiritual life should be practical and adaptable to one's present situation. He taught that it was precisely in the midst of a life full of distractions that one could best practice the little virtues, including kindness, gratitude, patience, optimism, humility, and gentle strength.

This book contains fifty-eight pieces of timeless wisdom from Saint Francis de Sales to help you live with authenticity and presence, deepen your spirituality, and serve others with love. Each excerpt from the 1600s was chosen because of its continued relevance in today's world. Accompanying each quote, you will find a reflection and a simple call to action for the day.

This book is intended to serve as a resource for inspiration and positive change. There is no proper order for reading the book; turn to whichever section speaks to your heart at the moment. Allow yourself time to sit with each passage, dwell on its meaning, relate its message to your present situation, and develop strategies to incorporate the teachings into your everyday actions.

chapter 1
be who you are
and
and
be that well

Let us be who we are
and be that well,
in order to bring honor
to the master craftsman
whose handiwork we are.

be self-loving

LOVE YOURSELF
wholly,
embracing and celebrating
the person God created you to be;
resist trying to fit in,
simply be yourself

TODAY
be who you are

Don't sow your desires
in someone else's garden;
just cultivate your own
as best you can;
don't long to be
other than who you are,
but desire to be
thoroughly who you are.

be authentic

LOVE YOURSELF
by cultivating your own hopes and dreams
rather than following a path
just to please others;
allow your words and actions
to reflect your true self,
letting go of worrying about
what others may think

TODAY
write your own story

We have to put up with others,
but first of all,
with ourselves,
and patiently accept
being less than perfect.
Good heavens, dear daughter,
what makes us think
that we can enter into a state
of interior rest
without going through
normal setbacks and struggles?

be patient

LOVE YOURSELF
by patiently accepting being less than perfect,
recognizing that setbacks and struggles
are part of your journey;
grant yourself
the same encouragement and support
you give your friends

TODAY
treat yourself
like a friend

Be patient
with everyone,
but above all
with yourself;
I mean,
don't be disturbed
about your imperfections....

be vulnerable

LOVE YOURSELF
by refusing to allow your imperfections
to disturb you or limit you,
reminding yourself that everyone is imperfect;
bravely share your humanness with others,
forming deeper connections

TODAY
show people
the real you

When we fall. . . .
Let us rise up
peacefully and quietly,
mend the broken net of love,
and go on with our work.
There is no need
to cast away your lute
or break its chords,
because it is
somewhat out of tune.
Listen attentively
till you find out
which is the faulty string,
and then raise
or lower it accordingly.

be optimistic

LOVE YOURSELF
by rising up from a fall,
peacefully and confidently,
focusing on your many unique talents
rather than your flaws;
allow yourself time to look inward,
listening attentively
to discover areas of self-improvement,
before making small adjustments
and carrying on with your work

TODAY
find the silver lining

So, you must choose:
is it better
that there should be
thorns in your garden
in order to have roses,
or that there should be
no roses
in order to have
no thorns?

be courageous

LOVE YOURSELF
by choosing
to step out of your comfort zone
and follow your creative passions,
daring to pursue a more fulfilling life;
embrace new experiences
with an adventurous spirit,
accepting the challenges you encounter
as opportunities to build character

TODAY
accept the thorns
in order to have roses

We should not be troubled
at finding ourselves
always novices
in the exercise of virtue. . . .
Instead of disturbing ourselves
because we have made
so little progress
in the past,
let us diligently strive
to do better
in the future.

be persevering

LOVE YOURSELF
by appreciating your dedication
to practicing the little virtues
in your everyday life
rather than being bothered
that you are always a novice;
view your efforts themselves
as signs of your progress,
reminding yourself that
everyone is a novice

TODAY
value the journey

When humility and meekness
are good and true
they preserve us
from the inflammation and swelling
that injuries usually cause
in our hearts.
If we are proud,
puffed up, and enraged
when we are stung and bitten
by detractors and enemies,
it is a sure sign
that in us
neither humility nor meekness
is genuine and sincere
but only
apparent and artificial.

be humble

LOVE YOURSELF
by remaining humble,
understanding that when you are
puffed up with pride,
your faults may cause you
greater embarrassment and discouragement;
reach out to others
for guidance and companionship,
believing that
life is not meant to be navigated alone

TODAY
do not be afraid
to ask for help

O dear daughter,
don't be examining yourself
to see if what you are doing
is little or much, good or bad. . . .
As much as possible,
do well what you have to do,
and once it is done,
think no more about it,
but turn your attention
to what has to be done next. . . .
Unless you do this,
your imperfections,
of which you are acutely conscious,
will disturb you even more
and thus grow stronger,
for nothing is more favorable
to the growth of these "weeds"
than our anxiety and overeagerness
to get rid of them.

be self-compassionate

LOVE YOURSELF
by calmly completing your work,
moving from one project to the next
without over-analyzing your actions;
let go of the need to be perfect,
simply do your best

TODAY
quiet your inner critic

Nothing
is so strong
as gentleness –
nothing
so gentle
and loving
as real strength.

be gentle and strong

LOVE YOURSELF
by protecting your inner peace,
resisting the urge to become defensive
or judgmental in stressful situations;
allow yourself time
to collect your thoughts,
pausing before you speak

TODAY
respond rather than react

It is sometimes necessary
for us to relax both mind and body
by some kind of recreation. . . .
Get out into the open air,
be entertained
by happy, friendly conversation,
play the lute
or some other musical instrument,
sing to musical accompaniment. . . .
All that is needed
is the common prudence
that gives due order, time,
place, and measure
to all things.

be balanced

LOVE YOURSELF
by connecting with others
through conversation and laughter;
spend time outdoors,
grateful for the immense beauty
and rejuvenating power of nature;
infuse your life with music,
feeling the notes and lyrics in your soul
as you sing, dance, and play

TODAY
have fun

First thing
in the morning,
prepare your heart
to be at peace;
then take great care
throughout the day
to call it back
to that peace frequently,
and, as it were,
to again
take your heart
in your hand.

be centered

LOVE YOURSELF
by making yourself a priority,
letting go of the need
to always say yes to others;
begin each day with a peaceful heart
and take great care throughout the day
to call it back to that peace frequently,
closing your eyes
and focusing on your breath

TODAY
unplug

chapter 2
love and respect others

Lose
no occasion,
however trifling,
of exercising
sweetness of heart
towards anyone.

be inclusive

SEEK CONNECTION
by embracing every opportunity,
no matter how small,
to show kindness to others;
welcome, include, and accept all people,
building a more diverse
and cohesive community,
one friendship at a time

TODAY
introduce yourself
to someone new

Love
begets
love;
and
true love
always carries
respect
with it.

be empowering

SEEK CONNECTION
by respecting all people,
valuing each person's feelings and rights
and affirming each person's worthiness;
help people to become their best selves,
believing that the entire community benefits
when the potential of each of its members
is appreciated and nurtured

TODAY
treat everyone
with respect

Hatred
separates us
and love
brings us together.

be considerate

SEEK CONNECTION
by being curious about others,
recognizing and appreciating
people as individuals;
take action to eliminate discrimination,
beginning with becoming aware
of your own biases
and working to overcome them

TODAY
believe we are all
in this together

It is a good practice
of humility,
never to look upon
the actions
of our neighbors,
except to remark
the virtues
that are in them,
but never
their imperfections.

be kindhearted

SEEK CONNECTION
by complimenting people
for their kindness, patience, and integrity
rather than pointing out their faults;
strive to find the goodness
in everyone you meet,
spreading optimism and joy
and inspiring others to do the same

TODAY
see the good
in everyone

One
can catch
more flies
with
a spoonful
of honey
than with
a hundred barrels
of vinegar.

be engaging

SEEK CONNECTION
by using your positive energy
to build relationships,
sharing your enthusiasm
and upbeat attitude with others;
get involved in your community,
actively working alongside others
to help create a better world

TODAY
be the light

The ways by which
we can unite ourselves
to our neighbor
are very numerous. . . .
Since God wants us
to love and cherish others,
we must see
our neighbor in Him.

be harmonious

SEEK CONNECTION
by loving and cherishing your neighbors,
remembering that everyone is a child of God;
reach out to those who are
stigmatized and marginalized,
seeing people in the hope of the wholeness
to which they were created

TODAY
see God in others

Be just and equitable
in all your actions….
Always put yourself
in your neighbor's place
and them in yours,
and then
you will judge rightly….
[E]xamine your heart often
to see if it is such
toward your neighbor
as you would like theirs to be
toward you
were you in their place.

be empathetic

SEEK CONNECTION
by asking your neighbors
about their feelings and needs
and truly listening to their answers,
valuing honest and sincere conversations
as the best means of better understanding
each person's perspective;
when your neighbors are in need,
offer them support rather than judgment,
showing them that you are with them

TODAY
open your heart
to others

Blessed
are the hearts
which can bend;
they shall never be broken.

be collaborative

SEEK CONNECTION
by maintaining an open mind
and a willingness to compromise
as you work with others to create change;
educate yourself
about community and global issues,
past and present,
allowing yourself to adjust
your assumptions and expectations
as you become better informed

TODAY
allow yourself to bend

One needs
a tender, kindly,
loving heart
towards one's neighbors,
particularly when
they are troublesome
or offensive to one,
because then
we love them
solely for God's sake –
a love all the worthier
that is free from
earthly motives.

be supportive

SEEK CONNECTION
by offering people kindness,
particularly when they are being
troublesome or offensive,
reminding yourself that
you do not know their whole story;
recognize that a person's behavior
is likely a reflection of what is going on
in that person's life
and has nothing to do with you

TODAY
believe people are doing
the best they can

Those who look carefully
into their consciences
are not very likely
to pass rash judgments.
Just as bees
in misty or cloudy weather
stay in their hives
to prepare honey,
so also
the thoughts of good people
do not go out in search of things
concealed among the cloudy actions
of their neighbors. . . .
It is the part of an unprofitable soul
to amuse itself
with examining the lives
of other people.

be nonjudgmental

SEEK CONNECTION
by recognizing that everyone is imperfect,
including yourself;
rather than spending your time
examining the lives of other people
in search of their faults,
focus your efforts on improving yourself

TODAY
remember you are only
in charge of yourself

As soon as you see
that you are guilty of a [wrong],
correct the fault right away
by an act of meekness
toward the person
you were angry with.
It is a sovereign remedy against lying
to contradict the untruth
upon the spot
as soon as we see we have told one.
So also,
we must repair our anger instantly
by a contrary act of meekness.
Fresh wounds
are quickest healed.

be accountable

SEEK CONNECTION
by taking ownership
of your behavior and choices
rather than blaming others;
if your actions have caused harm,
actively work to make things better,
repairing relationships and rebuilding trust,
understanding that
fresh wounds are quickest healed

TODAY
take ownership
of your actions

As one swallow
does not
make summer,
neither
does it necessarily follow
from one act of sin
that a person
is vicious.

be merciful

SEEK CONNECTION
by accepting people
for who they are right now
instead of judging them
by their past behavior;
show your faith in others,
believing that every person
can learn from their mistakes
and grow from their experiences

TODAY
give people
a fresh start

We must not be angry
with one another
on the way,
but rather
we must march on
as a band
of brothers and sisters
united in
meekness, peace,
and love.

be forgiving

SEEK CONNECTION
by letting go of your anger and your grudges,
freeing yourself from these weights;
grant yourself and others
the gift of forgiveness
with an open heart

TODAY
offer peace

chapter 3
do small things
with great love

To walk
in the spirit of faith,
implies not merely walking
by the light of faith,
but in the glowing warmth
of holy love,
which is
the life and soul of faith. . . .
It is not believing only –
it is doing.

be wholehearted

SERVE OTHERS
and grow in your faith
through both prayer and service;
both are integral parts
of your spiritual life

TODAY
grow spiritually
by believing & doing

Devotion is simply
that spiritual agility and vivacity
by which charity works in us
or by aid of which we work
quickly and lovingly. . . .
To be good
you must have charity,
and to be devout,
in addition to charity,
you must have
great ardor and readiness
in performing
charitable actions.

be devout

SERVE OTHERS
eagerly and lovingly,
believing that everyone is called
to live a devout life:
to love God and to do what is good

TODAY
use your gifts
to serve others

Great deeds
may not always
come our way,
but at all times
we can do
little deeds
with perfection,
that is,
with great love.

be kind

SERVE OTHERS
by offering small acts of kindness
throughout your day,
recognizing that great deeds
may not always come your way;
trust that your actions can be transformative
regardless of their size

TODAY
do small things
with great love

Don't miss
the opportunity
to perform
as many acts of gentleness
as you can –
and as frequently
as you can –
no matter how small
these acts may seem;
for as our Lord says:
To the person
who is faithful
in little things,
greater ones will be given.

be sincere

SERVE OTHERS
by showing your faithfulness
in the little things;
perform your everyday duties
with enthusiasm and gratitude,
embracing the opportunity
to show gentleness to others

TODAY
be faithful
in the little things

We must have great care
to serve God well
both in great, lofty matters
and in small, unimportant things.
With love,
we can capture God's heart
by the one
just as well as the other. . . .
Bear patiently
the slight injuries,
the little inconveniences,
the inconsequential losses
that daily come to you.
By means of such trifles as these,
borne with love and affection,
you will completely win God's heart.

be pleasant

SERVE OTHERS
by lovingly accepting
life's little inconveniences;
allow your cheerful attitude
to create a ripple effect,
spreading happiness
to those around you

TODAY
brighten the world
with your smile

Occasions
do not often present themselves
for the exercise of
fortitude, magnanimity,
and great generosity,
but meekness, temperance,
integrity, and humility
are virtues that must mark
all our actions in life.
We like sugar better than salt,
but salt is in more common
and frequent use.
We must always have on hand
a good supply
of these general virtues
since we must use them
almost constantly.

be virtuous

SERVE OTHERS
by practicing the little virtues
in your daily life;
pay attention
to the many opportunities
you are given each day
to show your true character

TODAY
let the simple virtues
guide all your actions

Charity
is both a means
and an end. . . .
It kindles
faith and hope.
Just as
the soul is the life
of the body,
charity is the life
of the soul.

be charitable

SERVE OTHERS
by donating your time and skills
to causes that are meaningful to you;
perform charitable acts
that benefit and inspire others
while filling you up,
recognizing the value of charity
as both a means and an end

TODAY
pay it forward

The mere performance
of a good deed is not enough,
unless it is done
in a spirit of love.
Love alone
gives substance, weight,
worth, and merit
to our good works
in God's sight,
and a trifling good action,
done for love of him,
is worth far more
than some great thing
in which that love
has a smaller share.

be heartfelt

SERVE OTHERS
in a spirit of love
rather than merely
out of a sense of obligation;
perform good actions,
no matter how small,
with love and purpose

TODAY
serve others
in a spirit of love

You learn
to speak by speaking,
to study by studying,
to run by running,
to work by working;
and just so
you learn
to love God and others
by loving.
All those
who think to learn
in any other way
deceive themselves.

be affectionate

SERVE OTHERS
by nurturing and strengthening
your friendships,
learning to love by simply loving;
allow yourself
to freely express affection to your friends,
showing your appreciation
for their companionship

TODAY
be a good friend

God looks
at the heart
and its intention
rather than
at the gifts
offered to him.

be thoughtful

SERVE OTHERS
with sincerity and presence,
letting your love shine through;
show kindness to others
because you genuinely care about them,
without drawing attention to yourself
or seeking accolades

TODAY
live your values

I have one thing
to tell you,
so, remember it well:
we are sometimes so busy being
good angels
that we neglect to be
good men and women. . . .
We mustn't think we can fly,
for we are like little chicks
who don't have wings yet.

be human

SERVE OTHERS
by understanding the value
your everyday duties have in themselves
and your ability to bring joy to others
by performing these simple tasks with love;
this is all that is asked of you

TODAY
resist trying to be perfect;
simply be human

chapter 4
speak to God
heart to heart

Truly,
the chief exercise
of [prayer]
is to speak to God
and to hear God speak
in the depths
of the heart. . . .
Eye speaks to eye
and heart to heart.

be spiritual

GROW SPIRITUALLY
through prayer,
speaking to God
and listening to God;
speak your words
from your heart
and receive God's words
in your heart

TODAY
speak to God
heart to heart

God is in all things
and all places.
There is no place or thing
in this world
where he is not truly present.
Just as wherever birds fly
they always encounter the air,
so also
wherever we go
or wherever we are
we find God present.

be faith-filled

GROW SPIRITUALLY
by recognizing God's presence
in all things and places;
wherever you are
and whatever you do,
God is with you

TODAY
recall God's presence

The nightingale
has no less love
for its song
when it pauses
than when it sings.
The devout heart
has no less love
when it turns
to external duties
than when it prays.

be passionate

GROW SPIRITUALLY
by showing intention and commitment
to both prayer and your everyday duties;
be assured you do not have to set aside
your current responsibilities
to live a spiritual life

TODAY
let your actions
reflect your faith

Don't waste time during prayer
trying to understand exactly
what you are doing
or how you are praying;
for the best prayer
is that which keeps us
so occupied with God
that we don't think about ourselves
or about what we are doing.
In short,
we must go to prayer simply,
in good faith,
and artlessly,
wanting to be close to God
so as to love him,
to unite ourselves to him.

be genuine

GROW SPIRITUALLY
by approaching prayer
with a sincere and humble heart,
simply wanting to be closer to God;
your prayers need not be long or eloquent,
they just need to come from your heart

TODAY
pray simply

Many people
neither wish nor dare
to think over and reflect on
the particular graces
God has shown them
because they are afraid that
this might arouse
vainglory and self-complacence. . . .
There is no need to fear that
knowledge of his gifts
will make us proud
if only we remember this truth,
that none of the good in us
comes from ourselves. . . .
On the contrary,
a lively consideration
of graces received
makes us humble
because knowledge of them
begets gratitude for them.

be thankful

GROW SPIRITUALLY
by reflecting upon
the many graces God has shown you;
recognize God's presence in your life
with humility and gratitude

TODAY
see God's work
in your life

Do not think
that God is further away from you
when you are in the midst
of the busyness
to which your vocation calls you
than he would be
if you were enjoying a tranquil life.
No, it is not tranquility
which brings him close to our hearts;
it is rather the fidelity of our love;
it is not the feeling we have
of his sweetness,
but the consent we give
to his holy will.

be loyal

GROW SPIRITUALLY
by finding God
in the midst of your busyness,
accepting with love,
whatever life brings;
resist thinking your spirituality
can only be strengthened
in the quiet moments of your day

TODAY
be open to how God
is asking you to serve

The length
of our prayers
should be in proportion
to the amount of work
we have to do.
And since
it has pleased God
to place us
in the kind of life
in which
we always have distractions,
we may have to get used to
shortening
our times of prayer.

be flexible

GROW SPIRITUALLY
by remaining dedicated yet practical,
allowing your prayers to be shortened
when you feel pulled in many directions;
God understands your demanding life,
for it is God who has placed you
in a life that is full of distractions

TODAY
weave short prayers
into your busy day

After you rise
from meditation
you must remember
the resolutions
and decisions
you have made
and carefully put them
into effect
on that very day.

be devoted

GROW SPIRITUALLY
by seeking opportunities
to carry out the resolutions and plans
you have discerned through prayer;
these decisions are considered
the great fruits of your meditation,
for God has guided you toward them

TODAY
turn your prayers
into actions

[F]requently [lift] your heart
to God. . . .
When you go for a walk,
often turn your thoughts
to God;
pray often and briefly. . . .

be inspired

GROW SPIRITUALLY
by turning to God
throughout your busy day
for inspiration and renewal,
praying often and briefly;
when you go for a walk,
lift your heart to God,
even for just a few moments

TODAY
take a walk
& talk to God

Be in mental solitude . . .
since you cannot
be in real solitude. . . .
Hear Mass in your heart
when you cannot
hear it elsewhere.

be meditative

GROW SPIRITUALLY
by taking a moment to quiet yourself
in the midst of your hectic life;
God can be found
in the rhythm of your heart,
no matter your surroundings

TODAY
be still & listen

chapter 5
live in the present moment

Do not look forward
to the mishaps of this life
with anxiety,
but await them
with perfect confidence
so that when they do occur,
God, to whom you belong,
will deliver you from them.
He has kept you up to the present;
remain securely
in the hand of his providence,
and he will help you in all situations.
When you cannot walk,
he will carry you.
Do not think about
what will happen tomorrow,
for the same eternal Father
who takes care of you today
will look out for you tomorrow and always.
Either he will keep you from evil
or he will give you invincible courage
to endure it.

be content

BE AT PEACE
by greeting each day
with assurance that God will help you
through whatever comes your way;
God will either protect you from harm
or give you invincible courage
to endure it

TODAY
let there be peace within

Let us
serve God well today;
He will provide
for tomorrow.
Each day
has its own burden
to bear;
do not worry
about tomorrow,
for the same God
who reigns today
will reign tomorrow.

be present

BE AT PEACE
by appreciating
the uniqueness of each day,
and the many opportunities you are given
to choose how to love and how to live;
allow yourself to fully experience
the present day
without worrying about the next

TODAY
believe each day
has its own purpose

God conserves this great world
in existence amid constant change
wherein day unceasingly turns into night,
spring into summer, summer into autumn,
autumn into winter, and winter into spring.
One day is never perfectly like another:
some are cloudy, some rainy,
some dry, and some windy. . . .
Everything may be in confusion
not only around us . . . but within us as well.
Our soul may be overwhelmed
with sorrow or joy,
with sweetness or bitterness,
with peace or trouble,
with light or darkness,
with temptation or repose,
with pleasure or displeasure,
with aridity or tenderness,
it may be scorched by the sun
or refreshed by the dew —
for all that, ever and always
our heart's point, our spirit, our higher will,
which is our compass,
must unceasingly look and tend
toward the love of God.

be unwavering

BE AT PEACE
by understanding there is a time
for both joy and sorrow,
light and darkness;
trust that each has value and purpose,
allowing you to discover your true strength
and reminding you
to always keep your spirit
pointed towards God

TODAY
appreciate
the seasons of your life

Direct your thoughts
to being very good
at [accepting where you are in life]
and to bearing the crosses,
little or great,
that you will find there.
Believe me,
this is the most important
and the least understood point
of the spiritual life.
We all love
what is according to our taste;
few people like
what is according to their duty
or to God's liking.
What is the use
of building castles in Spain
when we have to live in France?

be brave

BE AT PEACE
by accepting
the difficulties you face right now,
recognizing their benefit
in teaching patience and fortitude;
focus on the good in your life,
dismissing the temptation
to think your life would be better
if things were different

TODAY
embrace your life
wherever you may find yourself

In order
to journey steadily,
we must apply ourselves
to doing well
the stretch of road
immediately before us
on the first day of the journey,
and not waste time wanting to do
the last lap of the way
while we still have to make it through
the first.

be steadfast

BE AT PEACE
by addressing only those issues
immediately in front of you,
resisting your desire to be
further down the road
than where you have actually traveled;
understand the need to be fully present
to truly learn and grow from an experience

TODAY
believe that each part
of your journey has a purpose

I recommend to you
holy simplicity.
Look straight in front of you
and not at those dangers
you see in the distance.
As you say,
to you they look like armies,
but they are only willow branches;
and while you are looking at them
you may take a false step.
Let us be firmly resolved to serve God
with our whole heart and life.
Beyond that,
let us have no care about tomorrow.
Let us think only of living today well,
and when tomorrow comes,
it also will be today
and we can think of it then.

be untroubled

BE AT PEACE
by living with holy simplicity,
refusing to devote time and energy
to worrying about events
that may never occur;
think only of living today well,
having no care about tomorrow

TODAY
live in harmony
with the world

If it is out of love for God
that the soul seeks escape
from its troubles,
it will do so patiently, meekly,
humbly, and calmly
and look for deliverance
rather by God's providence
than its own efforts. . . .
Birds stay caught in nets and traps
because when they find themselves ensnared
they flutter about wildly trying to escape
and in so doing
entangle themselves all the more.
Whenever you urgently desire
to escape from a certain evil
or to obtain a certain good
you must be especially careful
both to put your mind at rest and in peace
and to have a calm judgment and will.

be trusting

BE AT PEACE
by calmly turning to God
when you feel anxious
rather than behaving
like a bird caught in a net
further ensnaring itself
while wildly trying to escape;
simply put your trust in God
and your mind at rest

TODAY
believe this too
shall pass

Don't let anxiety
take control of your heart;
each day will tell you
what you are to do.
You have already passed through
a number of trials
by the grace of God;
the same grace
will be there for you
in all the occasions to come,
and will free you
from difficulties and rough paths
one after the other
even if God must send an angel
to carry you over
the more dangerous steps.

be hopeful

BE AT PEACE
by approaching each day
with confidence,
reminding yourself
of the many obstacles
you have already overcome;
God was there for you in the past,
and God will be there for you
in the future

TODAY
feel the warmth
of God's grace

sources

De Sales, Francis. *Introduction to the Devout Life*. Trans. John K. Ryan. New York: Doubleday, 1989.

---. *Treatise on the Love of God*. 2 vols. Trans. John K. Ryan. Stella Niagara: DeSales Resource Center, 2007.

Francis de Sales, Jane de Chantal: Letters of Spiritual Direction. Trans. Peronne Marie Thibert, VHM. Selected and introduced by Wendy M. Wright and Joseph F. Power, OSFS. New York: Paulist, 1988.

Golden Counsels of Saint Francis De Sales. McCarthy, Mary Paula, VHM, and Mary Grace McCormack, VHM, editors. Trans. Peronne Marie Thibert. Monastery of the Visitation, 1994.

Letters to Persons in Religion. Translated and edited by Rev. H. B. Mackey, OSB. London: Burnes, Oates & Washbourne, 1908.

Practical Piety Set Forth by Saint Francis de Sales, Bishop and Prince of Geneva, Collected from His Letters and Discourses, and Now First Translated into English. London: Burns and Lambert, 1851.

The Spirit of S. Francis de Sales, Bishop and Prince of Geneva by Jean Pierre Camus, Bishop of Belley, Rivingtons, London, Oxford, and Cambridge 1872.

index of sources

GC—Golden Counsels (Page)
IDL—Introduction to the Devout Life (Part, Chapter)
LSD—Letters of Spiritual Direction (Page)
LPR—Letters to Persons in Religion (Book, Letter)
PP—Practical Piety (Part, Chapter)
SSFDS—Spirit of Saint Francis de Sales (Part, Chapter, Section)
TLG—Treatise on the Love of God (Book, Chapter)

Made in the USA
Coppell, TX
20 June 2021

57781485R00079